THE STORY OF
WORLD WAR I
COLORING BOOK

GARY ZABOLY

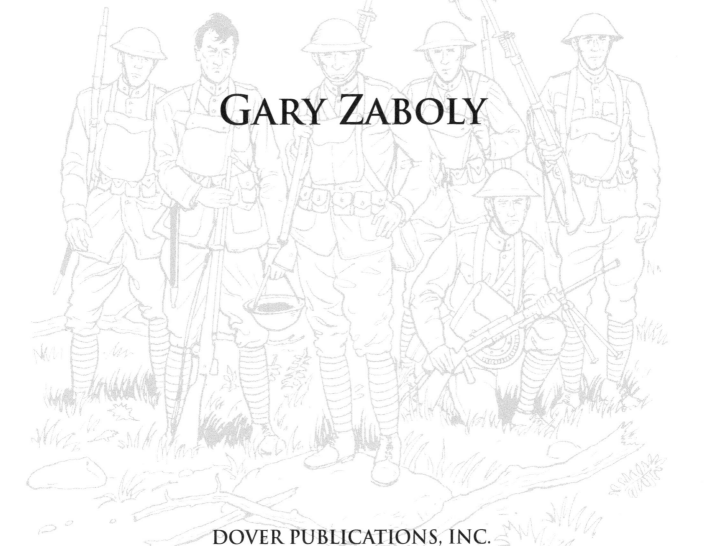

DOVER PUBLICATIONS, INC.
MINEOLA, NEW YORK

NOTE

From the assassination of Archduke Ferdinand in 1914—sometimes called "the shot heard 'round the world"—to the signing of the Treaty of Versailles in 1919, World War I is a fascinating time in world history. The illustrations and captions in this coloring book cover the politics of the war, as well as the battles and everyday living conditions of the soldiers. Well-known historical figures and events such as the Russian Revolution enrich this telling of the story of World War I—"the war to end all wars."

Bibliographical Note
The Story of World War I is a new work, first published by
Dover Publications, Inc., in 2013.

International Standard Book Number
ISBN-13: 978-0-486-49791-4
ISBN-10: 0-486-49791-7

Manufactured in the United States by LSC Communications
49791707   2017
www.doverpublications.com

1. Europe on the Eve of War. The early twentieth century was a time of peace and prosperity for the countries of Western Europe. There had been no wars for over four decades, and people were benefiting from advances in science and business. But the ambitions of the major European countries led to a drive to build the strongest army, the biggest navy, and the most advanced weapons. Alliances were formed: Great Britain with France and Russia, and Germany with Austria-Hungary and Italy. For ordinary European citizens, it was unthinkable that their leaders would go to war to resolve disputes.

2. The Assassination of Archduke Francis Ferdinand. The spark of war was lit in the early summer of 1914, in Sarajevo, Bosnia, a former Ottoman Turkish province that had been annexed by the Austro-Hungarian empire in 1908. The Bosnian Serbs wanted to join their kin in Serbia, and the Russians also rejected Austrian rule. Political extremists in Bosnia and Serbia included student Gavrilo Princip, who stood ready with bombs and guns when Archduke Ferdinand, heir to the Austrian throne, visited Sarajevo with his wife. On June 28, 1914, Princip shot them dead, and Austria sought revenge. Russia went to the aid of the Serbs, as did France. Germany then declared war on Russia and France. Soon England declared war on Germany. World War I had begun.

3. Marching Off to Battle. In every European army of 1914 there were still a few uniforms whose design went back to the 1700s, such as brass helmets with long plumes of horsehair and metal breastplates. The French infantry uniform was essentially unchanged since the Franco-Prussian War (1870–71): blue cap, greatcoat, and red trousers; the Zouaves were even more colorful in red Turkish caps and waistcoats, and red trousers. The German army wore gray uniforms, while Britain's Boer War (South Africa) experience had led to a practical khaki color. Most Europeans sent off their young men with parades and cheers, never suspecting that the coming war would destroy any old notions that war was "romantic."

4. The Marne. Germany's blueprint for the conquest of France, the Schlieffen Plan, called for a swift invasion of neutral Belgium, followed by a move southward into France's northern borders to entrap French forces in a broad sweep. The French and British armies rushed to meet this attack before it reached France, but they were pushed back in hard-fought battles to positions along the Marne River, not far from Paris.

Between September 5 and 10, 1914, the Allied armies regrouped and counterattacked, often taking advantage of gaps in the advancing German army. In one case, French soldiers were rushed to the battlefront in 600 Paris taxicabs to hold a critical point. The Germans halted, and both sides began strenghtening their positions by digging trenches, building forts, and laying down hundreds of miles of barbed wire. The cost in killed, wounded, and missing was enormous, with each side losing about a quarter of a million men.

5. The Introduction of Gas Warfare. A horrible new weapon was used on the battlefields of World War I: poison gas. The Germans first experimented with tear gas against the Russians in January 1915. In April, at the battle of Ypres in northwestern Belgium, German troops fired cylinders of yellow-green chlorine gas, killing hundreds of Allied troops within minutes and sending many more choking soldiers from their trenches. Respirators were eventually issued; even the dogs and horses wore them. Mustard gas and other chemicals would also be used as weapons by both sides during the remaining years of the war.

6. The Disaster at Gallipoli. As war in the trenches created a stalemate on the western front, Britain turned to the Middle East with the intention of knocking Turkey out of the war. This would help Russia and also establish a second front in southern Europe. First Lord of the Admiralty Winston Churchill planned the taking of the Gallipoli peninsula at the mouth of the Dardanelles Strait. But the British plan took too long, giving the Turks time to prepare their defense, and when the troops began to land in April 1915, a murderous fire rained on them from the cliff tops. Hundreds of English, French, and ANZAC (Australian and New Zealand) troops were killed. By November 1915, after more than 205,000 casualties, the Allies decided to remove the entire invasion force.

7. The First Tanks Used in Combat. As early as December 1914, the British began to develop an armored fighting vehicle, equipped with machine guns and cannon, that could break through enemy barbed wire, roll over trenches, and even knock down buildings. In September 1916, forty-nine Mark I "tanks" were sent to the front. At the First Battle of the Somme, these vehicles terrified many German troops, and some of the tanks managed to travel 3,500 yards before German shells stopped them. But the vehicles were slow and broke down often, and were virtually helpless if they fell into a trench.

The other major armies quickly began developing their own tanks. In Cambrai, France, on November 20, 1917, 320 British Mark V tanks got through the German Hindenburg line—the first mass tank assault in the history of war. At Amiens, in late summer, 1918, the Allies launched a major assault with 600 tanks and completely smashed the German positions. These early tanks, however, had many drawbacks: their crews suffered from smoke and the stench of oil and gasoline in almost total darkness and were subjected to constant rattling. In the summer, the temperature inside could go as high as 140° Fahrenheit.

8. Campaigns in the Alps. The Allies had promised to give Italy territory won in combat, and, in May 1915, the Italians broke from Germany and Austria-Hungary and declared war on them. The Italian army's offensive against Austrian troops in the Alps ended in failure. In 1918, the Austrians decided to conquer Italy without German help. But this time the Italian soldiers had help from French, British, and American troops, and they conquered the Austrians, taking 300,000 prisoners. Pictured are the elite mountain troops of Italy, "Alpini," scaling a rocky peak to surprise an Austrian position in one of the many numerous battles.

9. "They shall not pass!" The Battle of Verdun.
Determined to break through the French lines, the Germans, on February 21, 1916, launched a fiery attack of 80,000 heavy shells from 1,220 artillery pieces on the forts and trenches defending the city of Verdun. For the next ten months, the two armies battered one another. General Robert Nivelles declared, "They shall not pass!"—this became France's motto for the rest of the war. French infantrymen eventually retook the lost forts and pushed the Germans back to most of their original positions. Verdun did not fall, but the losses were huge: 542,000 Frenchmen and 434,000 Germans. Even today, live shells are found on farmlands and in forests.

10. The Battle of Jutland. For the first two years of the war, British navy ships had kept the German fleet from leaving the North Sea by blockading its two exits into the Atlantic. On May 31, 1916, in an attempt to break the blockade by destroying the British fleet, German Vice Admiral Reinhard Scheer sent a small decoy force of battle cruisers towards Norway, with the main German fleet following fifty miles behind them. The British took the bait: an advance group of battle cruisers and "dreadnoughts"—heavy battleships armed with big guns—confronted more than 100 German vessels moving in their direction.

But Admiral Sir John Jellicoe arrived shortly with the rest of the British fleet and opened up on the German warships by crossing the "T" of their oncoming path. Moving parallel to the German line, the British then attacked Scheer's fleet. Admiral Jellicoe tried to stay between Scheer's ships and his escape route. Darkness brought the main battle to a halt, although Scheer was able to push through the tail of Jellicoe's fleet and bring his battered warships back to port. The British lost fourteen vessels and 6,784 men, the Germans eleven ships and 3,039 men. The battle ended in a draw, but it convinced the Germans that they could not defeat Britain's Grand Fleet.

11. The Deadly Machine Gun. During the first months of World War I, both the Allies and the Axis powers were not aware how effective their newly developed machine guns would be in combat. As rows of attacking soldiers on both sides were mowed down, it was clear that fighting from the trenches would replace the old modes of direct combat. Essentially an American invention, the first true machine gun was the Maxim. The model shown here is the Maschinegeweher (MG)08, the German army's nearly direct copy of Hiram Maxim's original 1884 gun. Its range could reach up to 4,000 yards. In August 1914, the Germans had 12,000 MG08s. Fighting between trench lines in the face of machine guns set up in cross-firing positions generally was suicidal.

12. The Lafayette Escadrille. A handful of volunteer American pilots was welcomed by France's air service in 1914. By 1916 there were so many American pilots that they were organized separately as the Escadrille Américaine (American Squadron)—they later became Lafayette Escadrille. The men took part in history's first strategic bombing raid—the Mauser arms factory inside Germany—and engaged in frequent aerial combat with enemy planes. One of the fliers, Raoul Lufbery, scored seventeen enemy "kills" before being shot down. The squadron's insignia was the head of a Sioux chief, and a favorite aircraft was the Nieuport II, a single-seater biplane with a machine gun attached to the upper wing. After America entered the war, the corps was transferred to the U.S. Army Air Service.

13. The Battle of the Somme. As the battle for Verdun (France) raged on in July 1916, the Allies planned a major offensive on the Somme River. Eighteen British and sixteen French divisions attacked along a fifteen-mile front following an intense bombardment of the German positions. On the first day of the battle, 60,000 British soldiers were killed or wounded—the greatest one-day loss in the history of the British Army.

The French had better luck, breaking through part of the German lines. But the rest of those lines stood fast, and over the next four months the losses continued, with tanks, airplanes, and even horse cavalry attacking and counterattacking. By the end of the battle, only a little ground had been gained by the Allies, at a terrible price: 420,000 British, 195,000 French, and 650,000 Germans dead.

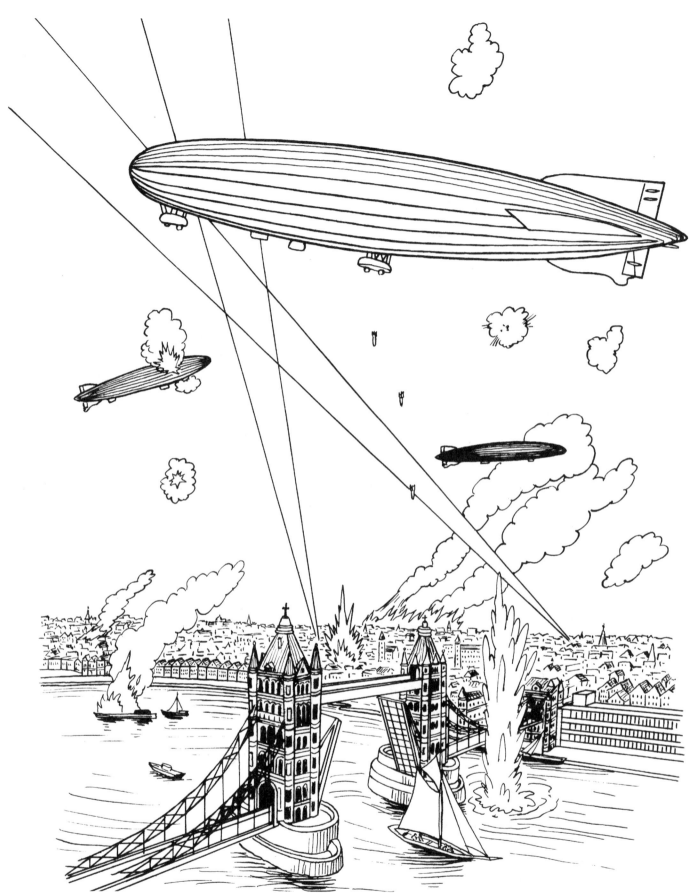

14. Giant Zeppelins Bomb London. Beginning in January 1915, the Germans, to break the will of the British, sent enormous Zeppelin airborne warships on bombing raids over England. Equipped with bombs, these warships made the first largescale attack on London on October 13. Later raids in 1916 caused many more civilian losses—550 by the end of the year—but the Zeppelins also began to be knocked out of the sky more often by antiaircraft fire and warplanes. Thus there were fewer raids over England in 1917 and 1918. Zeppelin storage areas in Germany were bombed by Allied planes as early as October 1914.

15. Mata Hari. The war's most famous spy was born Margaretha Geertruida Zelle in the Netherlands in 1876. By 1903, she was working as an artist's model and dancer in Europe. Eventually she adopted the stage name of Mata Hari. She became involved with influential Germans before the outbreak of the war and even attended a "spy" school in Germany. In France, she posed as a wealthy woman of fashion. Through her relationships with Allied officers, she obtained valuable military information, which she forwarded to the Germans. But French authorities had been watching her, and, in February 1917, she was arrested. The evidence against her was overwhelming, and in October she faced a French firing squad.

16. Pershing's Mexican Expedition. In January 1916, when Mexican revolutionary leader Pancho Villa was denied the sale of guns by the U.S. government, he executed sixteen American miners. He then raided the border town of Columbus, New Mexico, killing seventeen more Americans and looting and destroying much of the community. In March of that year, President Woodrow Wilson ordered Brigadier General John J. "Black Jack" Pershing and his forces into Mexico to "pursue and disperse" Villa's men. Pershing had 10,000 soldiers, mostly cavalry, under his command.

But Pancho Villa wanted to avoid a major battle, and Pershing could only draw out small bands of Villa's men into an occasional skirmish. But on one occasion, at Carrizal, American troops were overwhelmed by a larger force of Mexican regulars. At the ranch of one of Villa's men, Pershing's young aide, Second Lieutenant George S. Patton, shot down three bandits. In February 1917, after ten months of engagement, which scattered Villa's force and resulted in 400 casualties—Pershing's mission was ended.

17. Life in the Trenches. During the four years of battle along the western front in Europe, soldiers on both sides spent most of their time in trenches and dugouts—crude, dirty, and poorly lighted. Trenches without wooden bunks had sleeping shelves scooped out of the dirt walls. Many soldiers lost their lives due to trench foot, frostbite, rheumatism, and filthy conditions. Flooding was an almost constant problem. When not engaged in drills or battle, the men washed laundry, cleaned their weapons, conversed, sang, read, wrote letters and poems, or played cards, dice, or whist. Or they simply slept as much as they could.

18. The Red Baron. The most renowned air combat ace of 1914 to 1918 was Germany's "Red Baron," Captain Manfred Freiherr von Richthofen. He reportedly shot down 80 Allied planes, a record for the war. Born in 1892, he became a military cadet at 11 and a lancer cavalryman by 18. In 1916 he commanded the Richthofen Flying Circus, daredevil pilots like himself who enjoyed dogfights in the skies over the western front. They flew in red Fokker triplanes. Von Richthofen finally was shot down in April 1918. Here he wears the Blue Max, Germany's highest air-force medal.

19. The Sinking of the *Lusitania*. Germany adopted U-boat submarine attacks on all British surface vessels in early 1915—ships would be targeted without an advance warning that was required to evacuate the crew and passengers. The U.S. and other neutral nations protested, for such attacks were not only barbaric but also a threat to international trade. Americans were among the victims of Germany's policy.

On May 7, 1915, the British luxury liner *Lusitania,* at that time the largest passenger ship afloat, was torpedoed off the coast of Ireland by a U-boat. It sank in less than twenty minutes. A total of 1,200 men, women, and children were lost, among them 124 Americans. The incident was condemned in American newspapers, and many called for war. Official protests were made to the German leaders, and their lack of cooperation led to increasing ill will between the two governments.

20. President Wilson Declares War on Germany.
Almost two years passed after the *Lusitania* disaster before President Wilson, reacting to the many German actions against the neutral United States and the failure of diplomatic efforts, concluded that joining the war was the country's only choice. U-boat activity had increased, and three American vessels were sunk in March 1917. On April 2, 1917, President Wilson told the House of Representatives, "We will not choose the path of submission. . . . I advise that Congress . . . exert all its power and employ all its resources to bring the Government of the German Empire to terms and end the war." Congress adopted his resolution, and America was at war.

21. America Rallies to the Cause. Since many men were needed for its overseas army, the U.S. government passed a bill requiring military service on May 18, 1917. By June 5, 9,000,000 had registered. Military camps were built, and tents, uniforms, weapons, ammunition, tanks, planes, artillery, transport ships, and other sea and land vehicles were ordered. Posters featuring motion picture stars such as Douglas Fairbanks, Mary Pickford, and Charlie Chaplin encouraged Americans to buy Liberty Bonds to pay for the war. Morale was boosted by such songs as George M. Cohan's "Over There" and Irving Berlin's take on "Mademoiselle from Armentieres," which became popular on both the home and war fronts.

22. "Lafayette, We Are Here!" John J. Pershing, who had just been promoted to full general, was chosen to lead the American Expeditionary Force. Only four months after his Mexican expedition, on June 13, 1917, he arrived in France with some of the army. As the troops paraded through Paris, they were welcomed with enthusiastic cheers. Pershing paid his respects at the tomb of the Marquis de Lafayette, who had gone to George Washington's assistance during the American Revolution, and Pershing's aide, Colonel Charles E. Stanton, declared, "Lafayette, we are here!"

By the end of 1917, General Pershing commanded fewer than 175,000 American soldiers in France (some were black regiments that remained segregated from their white counterparts throughout the war). But more "doughboys" were needed, and by the end of the war nearly 1,400,000 U.S. troops had served in France. Pershing wanted none of his soldiers placed under the command of foreign officers, but, in times of need, sending troops with French and British units was unavoidable.

23. Collapse of the Russian Front. In 1914 the Russian army had defeated the Austrians and were pushing west, threatening the frontiers of Germany. Launching a series of counterattacks, the Germans forced the Russians back. In 1915 and 1916 there were German and Russian victories, along with another, even greater defeat for the Austrians. But close to 4.5 million Russians had been killed, wounded, or captured since the beginning of the war—mutinies followed in early 1917, while in Moscow the government of Czar Nicholas was torn apart by revolution. The Russian soldiers had had enough of fighting—they climbed out of their trenches and began the long trek homeward.

24. The Russian Revolution. The war had cost Russia much more than the enormous loss of life. At home there were shortages of food, fuel, and other needs. In the winter of 1916 to 1917, one of the harshest in memory, there were mass protests and strikes. The Russian army, including Cossack guards, was given the job of putting down the rebellion, and many demonstrators were killed. Czar Nicholas was forced to give up the throne, and a temporary government was created. In October 1917, the Bolsheviks, under Vladimir Lenin, seized power, laying the foundation for the Soviet state. While under arrest in distant Siberia, the Czar, his wife, and their five children were executed by order of the Bolsheviks on July 17, 1918.

25. Lawrence of Arabia Captures Aqaba. The British army, having been conquered at Gallipoli, was determined to defeat the Turks elsewhere in the Middle East. Many of the Arab desert tribes had already revolted against their Turkish occupiers, and young Lieutenant Thomas Edward Lawrence, a student of archaeology and an expert on the culture and politics of the Arabs, was sent by the British to advise the Arab leader Emir Faisal. The British wanted to seize the Red Sea port of Aqaba to set up an important supply base for both Arab and Allied forces.

But the British had no confidence in the plan, as it required crossing the vast, harsh Nefud Desert. T. E. Lawrence and some 500 camel-and-horse–mounted followers not only crossed the desert but also managed, on July 6, 1917, to capture Aqaba by attacking the town from its undefended landward side. Three hundred Turkish soldiers were killed and another 700 taken prisoner. Lawrence's reputation increased as he led the desert warriors in other raids and attacks on enemy trains, contributing to the end of Turkish rule in Arabia and Palestine.

26. Medical Care for the Soldiers. Each wartime army had a medical department and first-aid stations close to the battle, but so many casualties were sent to the main military hospitals that European hotels and other large buildings (not to mention ships and trains) often served as substitutes. The American Red Cross treated both U.S. and Allied troops, and 20,000 of its nurses were assigned to active duty during the war. They provided care and comfort for men suffering a wide variety of injuries, from lost limbs to shellshock. Some 330 female and 70 male Red Cross nurses became casualties of the war.

27. American Troops in the Trenches. General Pershing did not want the American armed forces to get bogged down fighting in trenches as the French and British had, but his troops needed training from Allied officers. In late October 1917, the first doughboys entered the lines in the southern part of the front. The soldiers spent a miserable winter there, seeing action only when the enemy made an occasional move. But even when the Allies moved forward in 1918, there would be no escaping trench life, with its mud, disease, monotony, and threat of snipers.

28. The Charge of the Australian Light Horse at Beersheba. British General Edmund Allenby administered the final blow to the Turks in the Middle East in 1918. In the previous year, he had captured Beersheba and Jerusalem by advancing east from Egypt. While planning his attack on Beersheba on October 31, 1917, he ordered his Desert Mounted Corps, which included both horse and camel cavalry, to seize the desert city's precious wells. The brigade of 800 Australian Light Horsemen volunteered for the job.

Brandishing their sword bayonets (they had no sabers), they swept across the desert in the long parallel lines of a traditional cavalry charge. The Turkish defenders opened fire with artillery and rifles, taking lives but not stopping the cavalrymen, who were soon among them, many fighting on foot. The wells were seized and the town captured, at the cost of 31 horsemen killed and 36 wounded. Seventy horses were dead. Said one trooper: "It was the horses that did it. Those marvelous bloody horses."

29. The Germans Begin Their Last Big Offensive. In March 1918, having drawn many of his troops from the now peaceful eastern front, General Erich Ludendorff planned a surprise attack against the Allies in the west. Leading this assault would be specially trained "shock" troops. On March 21, along a 60-mile front, German guns pounded British and French positions as the shock troops repeatedly pushed forward. The drive broke through 40 miles of Allied territory but began to lose effectiveness and its supply line was weakened. French Field Marshal Ferdinand Foch shifted his reserves to check the German advance. Each side suffered about a quarter of a million casualties.

30. The Marine Devil Dogs of Belleau Wood.
General Ludendorff was not done with his attacks. In May 1918, after assaulting the British with limited success in the north, he pushed towards the Marne River in the south. American troops were sent forward, and after a nineteen-day battle they helped the French drive the Germans back across the river. Then the U.S. 2nd Division, led by its Marine Brigade, launched a counterattack that pushed the Germans out of other positions, including 600-acre Belleau Wood. Clearing the trees of the enemy cost the Marines 8,000 men. Legend has it that the Germans, after this battle, dubbed the Marines *Teufelhunde*—"Devil Dogs."

31. The Lost Battalion. Following more failed German attacks, Marshal Foch planned a major Allied counterattack. One wing, under Pershing, would push north, bringing it into the Argonne Forest, which the Germans had heavily fortified. The 77th Division, most of its men drafted from New York City and neighboring areas, formed the left part of the advance. They began moving on September 29 but met with stiff opposition in the forest. On October 2, the soldiers again pressed forward, with 550 of them climbing to the top of a ravine past the enemy line. Alert Germans surrounded them with a murderous fire from rifles, machine guns, stick grenades, mortars, and flamethrowers.

But Major Charles W. Whittlesey, a lawyer in civilian life, kept his head and encouraged his men to beat back the German attacks. He also refused all German surrender demands. Then a series of shells from nearby U.S. artillery landed in their very midst. A carrier pigeon named Cher Ami succeeded in carrying a message from Whittlesey's back to headquarters, begging that the shelling be stopped—and it was. Not until five long days had passed was the "Lost Battalion," as it became known in newspapers, saved by an American breakthrough.

32. Sergeant York. Another high point for American arms was provided by Corporal Alvin C. York of the 82nd Division. Born in a Tennessee mountain log cabin in 1887, York was a superb marksman. He was also a pacifist; yet, when drafted, he willingly joined the war effort, and by October 1918, he found himself in one of the American assaults through the northern part of the Argonne. When his company was pinned down by enemy machine guns, York picked off many of the gunners and downed six bayonet-charging Germans with his Colt .45. The surviving machine gunners surrendered. York was promoted to sergeant. He was awarded three medals: the French Legion of Honor, the Croix de Guerre, and the Congressional Medal of Honor. In 1941 Gary Cooper dramatized his life in the movie *Sergeant York.*

33. Assaulting the Hindenburg Line. Once the Argonne Forest was cleared, the Franco-American armies pushed across the Meuse River; in the north, French, British, Belgian, and American soldiers attacked the main Hindenburg line. In both assaults, thousands of artillery pieces pounded the German positions before the tanks and infantry went at them.

One of the American-made guns, a 155mm Howitzer nicknamed "Calamity Jane" (shown above) fired the last American shot of the war. The German lines broke, and, unable to stem the massive tide, the soldiers were ordered to fall back. The Allies pressed on, breaking through everywhere, past scenes of great destruction made by their guns.

34. The Signing of the Armistice. Even before the Allies had begun the Meuse-Argonne Offensive in September 1918, General Ludendorff realized that the German army was living on borrowed time. He declared, "The war must be ended!" When the army collapsed in October, a request for an armistice—an end to the fighting—was sent to President Wilson. He replied that he would not negotiate with the military dictatorship ruling Germany. Meanwhile, mutinies, riots, and then revolution broke out within Germany itself. A Socialist government took power, and the Kaiser fled to Holland.

On November 8, a German delegation headed by a civilian leader, Matthias Erzbergen, along with representatives of Germany's military, met with Marshal Foch and other Allied officers inside Foch's railroad coach headquarters in France. The terms of the Armistice—that Germany must stop all fighting and leave France, Alsace-Lorraine, Belgium, and Luxembourg within fourteen days and surrender huge quantities of war supplies, among other demands— were eventually agreed to and signed on November 11, 1918. The hostilities were over!

EUROPE 1919-1929

NORWAY SWEDEN FINLAND
NORTH SEA ESTONIA
NORTH IRELAND DENMARK LATVIA
IRISH FREE STATE LITHUANIA
GREAT BRITAIN EAST PRUSSIA
NETH. U. S. S. R.
ENGLISH CHANNEL BELGIUM GERMANY POLAND
SAAR
LUX.
ATLANTIC OCEAN CZECHOSLOVAKIA
FRANCE SWITZERLAND AUSTRIA HUNGARY
RUMANIA
PORTUGAL ITALY YUGOSLAVIA
SPAIN ADRIATIC SEA BLACK SEA
CORSICA ALBANIA BULGARIA
SARDINIA GREECE
MEDITERRANEAN
SICILY TURKEY
AFRICA

35. The Treaty of Versailles. Throughout the first half of 1919, the victorious powers met at conferences to determine the political and economic fate of Germany, as well as aid for the war-ravaged countries. President Wilson dominated the conferences, urging that a Covenant for a League of Nations be formed. Shown attending the Paris peace conference are the "Big Four": (left to right) Britain's David Lloyd George, Italy's Premier Vittorio Emanuele Orlando, France's Premier Georges Clemenceau, and President Woodrow Wilson. On June 28, 1919, the treaty that officially ended World War I was signed at Versailles, France. Germany had to make large payments and give up much of its territory. These terms, a punishment for Germany's actions, would lay the groundwork for German discontent that would simmer until World War II, twenty years later.